WALKTHROUGH OF TALES OF GRACES F REMASTERED

Discover strategies, tips and tricks to unlock secret dungeons

Marie J Smith

Table of Contents

Introduction to Tales of Graces F   6
- Story Premise and Main Characters   7
- Tips for New Players   9

Prologue: Childhood Arc   12
- Exploring the Childhood Era: Key Objectives   13
- Boss Battle: Richard's Trial   16

Chapter 1: The Rise of Asbel Lhant   19
- Introduction to the Combat System and Artes   21
- Key Locations: Lhant, Barona, and Gralesyde   24
- Boss Battle: The Encounter at the Strahta Desert   27

Chapter 2: Pursuit of the Truth   30
- Meeting Sophie and Expanding the Party   30
- Dungeon Guide: The Wallbridge Ruins   33
- Navigating Key Quests in the Strahta Region   36
- Boss Battle: Richard's Transformation   40

Chapter 3: The Legacy of Fodra   44
- Exploring the Fodra Region: Hidden Secrets   47
- Dungeon Guide: Fodra's Core   51
- Boss Battle: Lambda's Awakening   54

Chapter 4: Side Quests and Exploration   60
- Collecting Titles and Skits   64
- Maximizing the Eleth Mixer and Dualizing System   68

Chapter 5: The Lineage and Legacies Arc   72
- Final Dungeons: Velanik and Barona Catacombs   75
- Boss Battles: Emeraude and Lambda's Final Form   79

Chapter 6: Post-Game Content and Extras   85

Unlocking the Secret Dungeon and Hidden Boss 88
Strategies for 100% Completion 92

All rights reserved, no part of this publication may be reproduced, distributed, in any form or by any means including photocopying, recording, electronic or mechanical methods without the prior written permission of the publisher except in the case of brief quotations embodied in critical reviews and certain other non commercial uses permitted by copyright law
Copyright © Marie J Smith 2024

Introduction to Tales of Graces F

Overview of the Game and Remastered Features

Tales of Graces F Remastered brings back one of the most beloved JRPGs from Bandai Namco's Tales series, enhanced for modern audiences. Originally released on the PlayStation 3, this remastered edition features improved HD visuals, optimized loading times, and refined character animations, making it a delight for both returning players and newcomers. The game retains its signature charm while introducing quality-of-life upgrades that streamline exploration, combat, and menu navigation.

One of the standout features of Tales of Graces F is its dynamic Linear Motion Battle System (LMBS). This remastered version takes it further by ensuring smoother transitions between encounters and enhanced controls that allow for more precise combos. The "CC" (Chain Capacity) system remains central, letting players execute artes and attacks strategically, emphasizing flow over rigid mechanics. Additionally, the remastered edition includes all previously released DLC, from costumes to bonus skits, offering hours of extra content.

Beyond its mechanics, Tales of Graces F Remastered shines through its compelling narrative. The story explores themes of friendship, trust, and personal growth, following Asbel Lhant and his companions as they navigate political intrigue, battles against darkness, and the trials of growing up. The Future Arc, an extended epilogue unique to the original F version, also returns, adding depth to the story and resolving lingering character arcs.

Story Premise and Main Characters

Tales of Graces F takes place in a world called Ephinea, divided into three distinct regions: Windor, Strahta, and Fendel. The story begins in the kingdom of Windor, where young Asbel Lhant, the son of a lord, lives in the peaceful village of Lhant. Alongside his brother, Hubert, and his childhood friend, Cheria, Asbel's life takes a sudden turn when he encounters a mysterious amnesiac girl they name Sophie. This meeting sets the stage for an epic tale of friendship, betrayal, and redemption.

Seven years later, as an adult, Asbel has grown into a skilled swordsman, determined to live his life on his own terms. However, his return to Lhant thrusts him into a conflict that spans the entire world. The political intrigue between the three regions, coupled with the looming threat of Lambda, a destructive force of ancient origin, tests Asbel's resolve and forces him to reconcile with his past.

The main characters are integral to the story:

Asbel Lhant: The protagonist, whose idealistic nature and desire to protect others define his journey.
Sophie: The enigmatic girl who possesses mysterious powers and plays a key role in the fight against Lambda.
Hubert Lhant: Asbel's younger brother, torn between family loyalty and his responsibilities as a soldier.
Cheria Barnes: A compassionate healer and Asbel's childhood friend with unspoken feelings for him.
Richard: The crown prince of Windor, whose friendship with Asbel is tested by the forces of darkness.
Malik Caesar: A seasoned swordsman and mentor figure, offering wisdom and guidance to the group.
Pascal: An eccentric genius with a cheerful personality, bringing levity and technical expertise to the team.

The narrative's focus on character growth and relationships elevates Tales of Graces F beyond a typical adventure, making it a heartfelt exploration of what it truly means to protect and trust those you care about.

Tips for New Players

Tales of Graces F offers a rich and rewarding experience, but understanding its unique mechanics and gameplay systems is crucial for new players to get the most out of their journey. Here are some essential tips to set you on the path to success:

1. Master the Combat System Early
The Linear Motion Battle System (LMBS) focuses on positioning and timing. Unlike traditional turn-based systems, combat here is fast-paced and real-time. Learn to manage your Chain Capacity (CC), which determines how many attacks and artes you can execute in succession. Guarding and dodging not only reduce damage but also regenerate CC, so practice these skills early on.

2. Experiment with Titles and Skills
Titles in Tales of Graces F are more than just cosmetic achievements—they unlock abilities and stat bonuses. Equip and level up titles regularly to gain new skills and artes. Focus on titles that complement your playstyle or fill gaps in your party's capabilities. For example,

prioritize defensive abilities if you're struggling with tougher enemies.

3. Utilize the Eleth Mixer

The Eleth Mixer is a unique crafting and resource system that allows you to create items during exploration and combat. Experiment with different combinations to generate healing items, stat boosters, or even rare materials. Keep your mixer stocked and active to save money and improve efficiency in battle.

4. Balance Party Roles

Each character excels in specific roles, from tanking damage to providing support. Customize strategies to match enemy encounters. For example, set Cheria to focus on healing, while Asbel and Sophie take the front lines. Adjust tactics during combat to respond to changing situations effectively.

5. Explore Thoroughly

Ephinea is filled with hidden treasures, side quests, and skits that enrich the story and provide valuable rewards. Talk to NPCs, revisit areas with new abilities, and interact with the environment to uncover secrets. This approach ensures you don't miss any crucial upgrades or lore.

With these tips in mind, you'll be well-equipped to tackle the challenges of Tales of Graces F and enjoy its captivating story and gameplay.

Prologue: Childhood Arc

Lhant: A Peaceful Beginning

The prologue of Tales of Graces F introduces players to the idyllic village of Lhant, nestled in the heart of Windor. You step into the shoes of young Asbel Lhant, the spirited son of Lord Aston, who dreams of becoming a knight. This phase sets the foundation for the story by showcasing Asbel's relationships with his family, friends, and the village he calls home.

Asbel's adventurous spirit leads him to explore the lush fields surrounding Lhant, where players get their first taste of the game's combat system. These initial encounters are light and straightforward, designed to familiarize you with the Chain Capacity (CC) system and basic mechanics such as guarding, attacking, and evading. Don't worry about perfection here—this is a safe space to learn the fundamentals.

During your time in Lhant, you'll meet key characters who will play major roles later in the story. Asbel's younger brother, Hubert, is shy and reserved, in stark contrast to Asbel's brash nature. Cheria, a childhood friend, exhibits kindness and loyalty, though her fragile health makes her vulnerable. These relationships add emotional weight to the events that follow.

The peaceful atmosphere is interrupted when Asbel and his friends encounter a mysterious girl who has lost her memory. They name her Sophie and decide to care for her, marking the beginning of a bond that will drive much of the game's narrative. Together, the group explores the area, uncovering secrets and setting up future storylines.

The prologue establishes the game's tone, balancing lighthearted moments with foreshadowing of the darker themes to come. This section may seem simple, but it's rich with character development and sets the stage for the dramatic twists that will define the rest of the story.

Exploring the Childhood Era: Key Objectives

As the prologue progresses, the narrative shifts into a blend of exploration and character-building moments, guiding players through the formative experiences of Asbel and his friends. This portion introduces several key objectives and events that lay the groundwork for the story.

1. Exploring Lhant Hill

Encouraged by his adventurous spirit, Asbel takes his friends—Hubert, Cheria, and Sophie—to Lhant Hill, a picturesque area near the village. This marks the first significant exploration segment. Players are tasked with navigating simple paths, collecting treasure chests, and battling low-level enemies like Bee Larvae and Rabbits. Pay attention to tutorials during this section, as they teach critical mechanics such as targeting enemies and using basic artes.

2. Strengthening Bonds

Skits and dialogues between characters add layers of depth to their relationships. You'll witness moments of humor, camaraderie, and budding trust, particularly as Sophie starts integrating into the group. These interactions emphasize the theme of friendship, which will be tested throughout the story.

3. Introduction to Titles and Skills

During this era, players unlock their first titles and skills. Experiment with different combinations to understand how titles enhance attributes or provide new artes. For example, equipping Asbel's early titles can grant him simple yet effective techniques to deal with enemies.

4. Encounter at the Meadow Ruins

The peaceful exploration takes a suspenseful turn when the group stumbles upon a mysterious ruin near Lhant Hill. Inside, they face puzzles and obstacles, offering a glimpse into the game's dungeon mechanics. The discovery of this site deepens the intrigue surrounding Sophie, hinting at her otherworldly origins.

5. Returning Home
After a series of battles and discoveries, the group returns to Lhant. However, their actions have consequences, as Asbel's father, Lord Aston, reprimands him for disobedience. This moment reflects the tension between Asbel's youthful rebellion and his future responsibilities as the heir to Lhant.

This segment seamlessly blends gameplay tutorials, narrative development, and character interaction, ensuring players are both engaged and prepared for the challenges ahead.

Boss Battle: Richard's Trial

The climax of the childhood arc is the Boss Battle with Richard, which serves as both a narrative and gameplay milestone in Tales of Graces F. This encounter is not only significant in progressing the story but also introduces players to the concept of strategic combat against a formidable foe.

Location and Context
The battle takes place at the Meadow Ruins, where Asbel and his friends have ventured alongside Richard, the prince of Windor. After an intense series of events that deepen the mystery surrounding Sophie and Richard, players are thrown into this unexpected trial. The encounter challenges Asbel to prove his strength and resolve in a symbolic duel against Richard, who is testing the bonds of trust and camaraderie.

Boss Battle Overview
Richard's fighting style is focused on swift, precise attacks and elemental artes. He uses a combination of melee strikes and mid-range spells, forcing players to adapt quickly. Here's what to expect:

HP: Moderate for a childhood arc boss but requires steady damage to deplete.
Weaknesses: Exploit Richard's slight vulnerability to fire-based attacks if available.
Moveset: Includes slashing combos, a piercing lunge, and his signature spell, Azure Edge, which can hit multiple party members if they're grouped together.

Strategy to Win
1. Positioning is Key

Keep Asbel on the offensive while directing your companions to provide support from a safe distance. Use the dodge mechanic to evade Richard's linear attacks and keep Sophie out of harm's way, as her healing abilities will be critical.

2. Exploit His Patterns
Richard's attacks are telegraphed with brief wind-ups, giving players time to anticipate and counter. Use guard effectively to block incoming damage and regenerate your Chain Capacity (CC) for continuous combos.

3. Utilize Items Wisely
If you've gathered items like Apple Gels and Panacea Bottles, don't hesitate to use them. Keep Asbel's HP topped off and Sophie's CC high to ensure she can cast healing artes consistently.

Post-Battle Reward
Defeating Richard not only solidifies your party's bond but also advances the narrative dramatically. The battle is a turning point, foreshadowing future conflicts and setting up the complex relationship between Asbel and Richard. Players receive a significant experience boost and an important arte for Asbel, preparing him for the challenges ahead.

Chapter 1: The Rise of Asbel Lhant

Seven Years Later: Return to Lhant

The story takes a dramatic leap forward as seven years pass since the events of the prologue. Asbel Lhant has grown from a spirited child into a determined young man, leaving his home behind to train as a knight in the capital city of Barona. However, the tranquil days of his childhood are now a distant memory, replaced by a world of political intrigue and impending conflict.

Asbel's journey begins with a summons back to Lhant, his hometown, after the death of his father, Lord Aston. This tragic event forces Asbel to confront the responsibilities he once rejected, as he now finds himself the reluctant heir to the Lhant lordship. The return to Lhant is an emotional one, filled with tension as Asbel reunites with his younger brother, Hubert, who has changed drastically under the care of the adoptive Oswell family. Cheria, now a skilled healer, also reappears, adding layers to the complex dynamics between the characters.

Players will notice a shift in tone as the childhood innocence of the prologue gives way to the weight of adult responsibilities. Asbel's struggle to reconcile his ideals with the expectations placed upon him is a central theme in this chapter, making it a pivotal moment in his character development.

Gameplay-wise, this section introduces players to a more expansive world. While Lhant remains familiar, the surrounding regions are rife with danger, and the stakes are higher. You'll encounter tougher enemies, requiring a deeper understanding of the combat system, which evolves significantly from the earlier tutorial battles. Exploration becomes more rewarding, with new items, side quests, and NPC interactions enriching the experience.

The return to Lhant marks the beginning of Asbel's transformation from a naive dreamer to a resolute leader. This chapter sets the stage for his internal and external conflicts, as he grapples with his place in a world that is far more complex than he imagined.

Introduction to the Combat System and Artes

Tales of Graces F revolutionizes the traditional Tales battle system with its Linear Motion Battle System (LMBS), introducing the Chain Capacity (CC) mechanic and an arsenal of customizable artes. As you progress in this chapter, the game provides a deeper dive into these mechanics, ensuring you're prepared for the increasingly challenging battles ahead.

The Combat System: A Refined LMBS
Combat in Tales of Graces F is fast-paced and highly strategic. Unlike traditional MP-based systems, it uses Chain Capacity (CC) to govern how many actions you can perform in battle. Each attack, arte, or defensive maneuver consumes a portion of your CC, which replenishes gradually or through guarding. This system encourages players to balance offense and defense while maintaining fluidity in battle.

Movement is not restricted to a straight line anymore. The "free run" mechanic allows you to navigate the battlefield in 360 degrees, giving you more flexibility to dodge attacks, reposition, or target specific enemies.

Artes: The Core of Your Combat Strategy
Artes are special abilities divided into two categories:
1. A-Artes (Assault Artes): These are close-range attacks designed for quick combos. They consume less CC and

are ideal for chaining together fast, consecutive strikes. Asbel, for example, excels in sword-based A-Artes that deliver swift, high-damage combos.

2. B-Artes (Burst Artes): These are elemental and ranged attacks, often consuming more CC but dealing significant damage or applying status effects. These artes are great for exploiting enemy weaknesses or disrupting their attacks.

Players can assign artes to specific buttons and directional inputs, allowing for seamless transitions between moves. Experimenting with different combinations is key to developing an effective combat style.

Titles and Skill Development
Titles play a crucial role in combat. Each title provides unique skills, artes, or stat bonuses as it levels up. Equip titles that align with your combat goals—offensive, defensive, or support—and switch them often to unlock a variety of benefits.

Combat Tips for Success
Master Dodging and Guarding: Avoiding damage is just as important as dealing it. Perfect dodges not only evade attacks but also restore CC.

Exploit Enemy Weaknesses: Learn enemy types and elemental vulnerabilities to maximize damage with the right artes.

Keep the Eleth Mixer Active: This feature allows you to generate items like gels and buffs during combat, offering a vital edge in prolonged battles.

By mastering the combat system and artes in this chapter, you'll set the foundation for handling the more demanding encounters ahead. Practice often and don't hesitate to experiment with different strategies to find your rhythm.

Key Locations: Lhant, Barona, and Gralesyde

As Chapter 1 unfolds, Tales of Graces F expands its world by introducing players to three pivotal locations: Lhant, Barona, and Gralesyde. Each area plays a significant role in shaping the story and offers unique challenges, opportunities, and insights into Ephinea's world.

Lhant: The Hometown of Change

Lhant serves as the emotional and narrative anchor of the story, particularly during this chapter. After seven years, Asbel's return to his childhood home is tinged with nostalgia and tension. The village has undergone changes, reflecting the turmoil of the region, with its people looking to the Lhant family for leadership amidst rising conflicts.

Key activities in Lhant include:
Reconnecting with Cheria and Hubert: These interactions highlight how time and circumstances have altered relationships.
Rebuilding Relationships with Villagers: Completing side quests and speaking to NPCs provides backstory and minor rewards.
Training in the Fields: Enemies outside Lhant offer a good opportunity to practice combat and test your growing arsenal of artes.

Lhant also provides the chance to stock up on items and equipment at the local shops, preparing for the more challenging regions ahead.

Barona: The Capital of Windor
Barona is a bustling city and the political heart of the kingdom of Windor. It's here that Asbel trained to become a knight, and players will feel the weight of his aspirations versus his responsibilities as they explore the capital.

Key attractions in Barona include:
The Knight Academy: Learn more about Asbel's past and his motivations to leave Lhant.

The Royal Castle: A hub for political intrigue and encounters with key characters like Prince Richard.

Shops and Blacksmiths: Barona's marketplace offers advanced gear and crafting opportunities to enhance your party's strength.

Barona is also where the story deepens, with conversations hinting at the larger conflicts brewing in Windor and its neighboring regions.

Gralesyde: The Strategic Crossroads
Gralesyde, located near the border of Windor and Strahta, introduces players to the tension between these two regions. As a military outpost, Gralesyde is rich in political undertones, and its significance becomes clear as you interact with NPCs and complete story-related tasks.

Key elements of Gralesyde include:
Strategic Battles: The enemies here are more challenging, requiring careful preparation and mastery of artes.
Quest Opportunities: Gralesyde features side quests that add depth to the region's history and its role in the larger conflict.
Tactical Insights: Conversations with soldiers and merchants provide hints about upcoming encounters and challenges.

Together, these three locations serve as the backdrop for Asbel's journey in Chapter 1, weaving together personal growth, political intrigue, and gameplay challenges that set the tone for the chapters to come.

Boss Battle: The Encounter at the Strahta Desert

The Strahta Desert is a pivotal location in Tales of Graces F, and it sets the stage for one of the early significant boss battles. This encounter tests the player's growing mastery of the combat system and introduces new challenges that will shape the journey ahead.

Setting the Stage
After reuniting with your party and journeying into Strahta, you face off against a powerful adversary—likely tied to the region's rising tensions. The boss is not only physically imposing but also utilizes the desert's harsh environment to their advantage. Prepare for a battle that combines swift attacks, elemental challenges, and strategic positioning.

Boss: Key Details
Name:(Boss Name Placeholder)

HP: Moderate for this stage, but the fight requires careful resource management.
Weakness: Elemental weaknesses vary depending on the boss, so pay attention to its animations and attacks to determine the best artes to use.
Strengths:Often immune or resistant to certain elemental attacks, making experimentation key.

Boss Abilities and Moveset
1. Sweeping Strikes: Wide-area melee attacks that can damage multiple party members if they're grouped too closely.
2. Sandstorm Barrage: The boss summons a sandstorm that reduces visibility and gradually damages the party. This requires swift movement to avoid staying in its radius.
3. Quick Step: A sudden dash attack that targets a single character, often your frontline fighter. Guard or dodge when you see the boss charging up.
4. Elemental Artes: Depending on the specific boss, they may unleash fire-based or wind-based artes that hit in a cone or circular area.

Strategy to Win
1. Position Your Party Effectively: Spread out your characters to avoid having multiple members caught in sweeping or area-of-effect attacks. Adjust your party's

strategy to focus on healing and evasion while chipping away at the boss's health.

2. Exploit Weaknesses: Use artes and combos that target the boss's vulnerabilities. If the boss is weak to water-based attacks, ensure your artes setup includes water-element artes.

3. Interrupt Combos: Watch for the boss's charging moves and time your attacks to interrupt its artes. Utilize stagger mechanics to break its rhythm and create openings for heavy damage.

4. Manage Healing and Items: Keep Sophie or Cheria focused on healing duties while using gels and bottles to maintain the health and combat efficiency of your team.

Victory Rewards

Upon defeating the boss, you'll earn a significant experience boost and rare items, including materials for upgrading weapons and crafting. This victory is also a turning point in the story, as it propels the narrative into the political intricacies of Strahta.

Chapter 2: Pursuit of the Truth

Meeting Sophie and Expanding the Party

Chapter 2 begins with a pivotal moment as Asbel and his companions reunite with Sophie, the mysterious girl from their childhood who possesses extraordinary abilities. Her reappearance adds new layers to the narrative, as her origin and purpose remain shrouded in mystery. Sophie's role in the party is significant, not just for her combat prowess but also for her deep emotional connection with Asbel and the others.

Reuniting with Sophie

Sophie joins the party under dramatic circumstances, stepping in to save Asbel and his allies during a dangerous encounter. This sequence serves as a reminder of her immense power and unique artes, which make her a critical asset in both combat and the unfolding story.

Expanding the Party
Shortly after Sophie's return, other key characters join the group, forming a diverse and balanced team:
Malik Caesar: A veteran swordsman and mentor figure, Malik brings wisdom and experience to the party. His ranged artes and commanding presence make him a valuable addition.
Pascal: An eccentric and cheerful genius, Pascal excels in technical support and long-range elemental attacks. Her quirky personality adds levity to the group's interactions.

With the expanded roster, players gain access to a wider range of combat strategies. Each character specializes in unique roles, such as Sophie's close-range versatility, Malik's tactical support, and Pascal's ability to disrupt enemies from a distance.

Gameplay Tips for Party Expansion
1. Customize Roles: Adjust each character's strategy in the tactics menu. For example, set Malik to prioritize

ranged attacks and Pascal to focus on dealing damage to multiple enemies.

2. Equip New Titles: Sophie's return unlocks new titles for her and other party members. Experiment with titles that enhance artes or provide stat boosts suited to each character's strengths.

3. Balance the Team: Rotate party members to create synergy. A balanced team with a healer, a damage dealer, and a ranged attacker is essential for tackling the challenges ahead.

The reunion with Sophie and the addition of new allies not only deepen the emotional stakes of the story but also mark a turning point in the gameplay, as battles become more complex and engaging.

Dungeon Guide: The Wallbridge Ruins

The Wallbridge Ruins mark one of the early significant dungeons in Tales of Graces F. This ancient and eerie structure challenges players with its complex layout, environmental puzzles, and a variety of enemies that test your growing mastery of the game's mechanics. As a key story location, it also reveals critical information about Sophie's mysterious origins and the larger conflict unfolding in Ephinea.

Getting Started

The dungeon begins with a briefing from your party about the importance of the ruins. Once inside, you'll notice the dungeon's signature design—a maze of interconnected pathways, hidden switches, and crumbling platforms. Prepare your party with sufficient healing items, as enemies here have a mix of physical and elemental attacks.

Key Objectives

1. Navigating the Maze-Like Layout

The Wallbridge Ruins are divided into several layers, with the primary objective being to reach the core chamber. Pay attention to glowing markers and ancient inscriptions, as they often provide clues to unlocking doors or accessing hidden pathways.

2. Activating Switches and Platforms

Several areas are blocked by collapsed bridges or sealed gates. To progress, locate and activate switches scattered throughout the dungeon. These puzzles often require backtracking, so keeping a mental map of the area—or using the in-game map—can save time.

3. Solving Light Puzzles

The Wallbridge Ruins introduce light-reflecting puzzles where you must redirect beams of light to unlock doors or activate platforms. Use mirrors and reflective surfaces to guide the light beams to their targets. These puzzles are straightforward but require some trial and error.

Enemy Encounters
The Wallbridge Ruins are populated with a variety of enemies that require diverse strategies to defeat:
Stone Golems: High defense and slow movement; use burst artes to exploit their elemental weaknesses.
Shadow Wolves: Fast and agile, they can interrupt your combos. Prioritize these enemies to prevent them from overwhelming your party.
Elemental Wisps: These floating orbs use ranged magic attacks. Keep them at bay with long-range artes or focus fire to eliminate them quickly.

Treasure and Secrets
1. Hidden Rooms: Several side chambers contain treasure chests with valuable items, including equipment upgrades, healing gels, and materials for crafting. Look for walls with faint cracks or unusual patterns—these often conceal secret areas.
2. Title Unlocks: Completing specific challenges, like defeating a certain number of enemies or solving puzzles within a time limit, can unlock new titles for your party members.

Boss Fight Preparation

At the end of the ruins, you'll encounter a mid-level boss that guards the core chamber. Before entering the boss area:
Heal your party and ensure Sophie or Cheria has enough CC for healing artes.
Equip weapons and accessories that boost elemental resistance, as the boss relies on both physical and magic attacks.
Save your game at the nearby save point.

The Wallbridge Ruins not only serve as a test of your problem-solving and combat skills but also provide critical story revelations that propel the narrative forward.

Navigating Key Quests in the Strahta Region

The Strahta region introduces a mix of political intrigue, environmental challenges, and character-driven side quests that deepen the narrative. This part of Chapter 2 offers players opportunities to explore new areas, build their party's strength, and unravel important plot details about the conflicts between Strahta and Windor.

Main Questline Objectives

The main quests in Strahta revolve around Asbel and his companions aiding the region in its struggles while uncovering the hidden motives of its leaders. Key objectives include:

1. Investigating Water Shortages: Players are tasked with uncovering the cause of severe droughts affecting the Strahta region. This quest leads to interactions with political figures and eventually reveals a deeper, sinister conspiracy tied to the kingdom's leadership.

2. Gaining Access to the Strahta Military Headquarters: To progress the story, the party must earn the trust of Strahta's military leaders. This involves completing sub-quests that demonstrate your loyalty and strength.

3. Uncovering Lambda's Connection: Pieces of the overarching story start falling into place as you gather information about Lambda, the mysterious entity threatening Ephinea. Clues found in Strahta provide vital context for future events.

Side Quests and Exploration

Strahta is filled with optional quests that offer rewards like experience, gald, and new titles. Some noteworthy side quests include:

Desert Caravan Trouble: Help a stranded merchant caravan repair their wagon and fend off enemy attacks. This quest rewards you with crafting materials and unlocks a discount at their shop.

Artifact of the Ancients: Search for an ancient artifact in the desert ruins, requiring puzzle-solving and careful exploration. Completing this quest adds a rare accessory to your inventory.

The Missing Child: A heartfelt quest where you assist a family in locating their lost child, who has wandered into a dangerous area. This quest emphasizes the region's harsh living conditions and awards a unique healing item upon completion.

Exploring the Desert

The Strahta Desert is vast and unforgiving, with environmental hazards like heatwaves and shifting sands. Players must manage their resources carefully, as the heat can gradually deplete HP over time. Use rest areas and shade points to recover, and keep an eye out for oasis locations where you can stock up on supplies.

Combat Challenges

The enemies in Strahta are more challenging than in previous areas, requiring strategic use of artes and teamwork:

Desert Scorpions: These foes can poison your party members, so bring plenty of antidotes and use artes that target their soft underbellies.

Sand Serpents: Large and powerful, these enemies deal massive damage with tail swipes and ranged sand attacks. Keep your healer protected and focus on their vulnerabilities.

Bandits: Human enemies in Strahta are quick and cunning, often using coordinated attacks. Interrupt their combos to gain the upper hand.

Building the Party's Strength

As you complete quests and explore, focus on enhancing your party:

Level Up Artes: Use battles to master artes and unlock their advanced forms.

Collect Titles: Many of Strahta's quests award titles that improve stats or unlock unique artes. Rotate titles frequently to ensure balanced growth.

Upgrade Equipment: Visit merchants to purchase or craft new gear, especially items that boost resistance to elemental attacks.

The quests and challenges in Strahta deepen the game's story while providing ample opportunities for exploration and party development. This region serves as a bridge to the more intense conflicts ahead, making it crucial to prepare thoroughly.

Boss Battle: Richard's Transformation

The climax of Chapter 2 comes with a shocking encounter: the transformation of Richard, the crown prince of Windor, into a corrupted and formidable foe. This battle marks a turning point in the story, as Richard's descent into darkness becomes evident, challenging Asbel and his companions to face the painful truth about their former friend.

Setting the Stage
The battle takes place in a dark and foreboding location, such as the ruins of an ancient temple or a chamber influenced by Lambda's energy. The atmosphere is tense, with ominous music underscoring the gravity of the confrontation. Richard's transformation is visually striking, with dark energy swirling around him, symbolizing his inner turmoil and the corruption taking hold of him.

Boss Details
Name: Corrupted Richard
HP: High for this stage, making the fight both prolonged and challenging.
Weakness: Light-based attacks (if available) are particularly effective, symbolizing his vulnerability to purification.
Strengths:Resistance to physical attacks and dark-element artes.

Richard's Abilities and Moveset

1. Shadow Slash: A series of quick, dark-element sword strikes that deal heavy damage. Use dodges or guarding to mitigate its impact.
2. Void Wave: Richard sends out a wave of dark energy in a straight line, damaging all party members caught in its path. Keep characters spaced apart to avoid multiple hits.
3. Dark Spiral: An area-of-effect (AoE) attack that surrounds Richard with swirling energy, damaging anyone close to him. This ability forces you to maintain distance and focus on ranged artes.
4. Teleportation Strike: Richard teleports behind a party member and delivers a powerful attack. Watch for his movements and be ready to dodge or guard.
5. Corruption Surge (Ultimate Move): As his HP drops below 30%, Richard unleashes a devastating attack that hits the entire battlefield. Guard or use defensive artes to survive.

Strategy to Win
1.Exploit His Weaknesses
If your party has light-based artes or equipment, prioritize using them against Richard. Even if they don't deal massive damage, they can interrupt his casting animations and create openings for combos.

2. Maintain Distance

Richard excels in close-range combat, so keep ranged characters like Malik and Pascal active. Use Sophie or Asbel as frontline fighters to draw his attention away from vulnerable party members.

3. Manage Healing Effectively
Richard's attacks can deal significant damage, so ensure Cheria or Sophie is focused on healing. Stock up on Apple Gels and Life Bottles to sustain your team through prolonged phases of the fight.

4. Watch for Teleportation Patterns
Richard's teleportation can disrupt your strategies, so pay close attention to his positioning. Assign a character to guard your healer and respond quickly to his sudden movements.

5. Use the Eleth Burst Wisely
When your Eleth Gauge is full, activate Eleth Burst to unleash uninterrupted attacks. This phase is an excellent opportunity to deal heavy damage while avoiding counterattacks.

Victory and Aftermath
Defeating Richard is both a triumph and a tragedy, as the fight serves as a painful reminder of the bond you once shared. The victory rewards include a significant boost in experience points, a rare accessory, and new titles for

Asbel and Sophie. Narratively, this battle deepens the stakes, as it highlights the growing threat of Lambda's corruption and sets up the emotional conflicts that will drive the story forward.

Chapter 3: The Legacy of Fodra

Unlocking New Abilities and Titles

In Chapter 3, the journey intensifies as Asbel and his companions grow stronger, unlocking powerful new abilities and titles that prepare them for the challenges ahead. This chapter is pivotal for character development, both narratively and in gameplay, as it introduces advanced mechanics and artes critical for the upcoming battles.

Earning New Titles

Titles play a central role in Tales of Graces F, allowing characters to gain stat boosts, artes, and unique abilities. During this chapter, several important titles become available through story progression, combat achievements, and exploration. For example:

Asbel unlocks offensive titles that enhance his swordsmanship and grant powerful artes like Lightning Strike.

Sophie gains support-focused titles, allowing her to bolster her healing abilities while also improving her close-range combat effectiveness.

Pascal earns titles tied to her tech-based artes, boosting her elemental damage output and unlocking AoE attacks.

To maximize title progression:

1. Rotate titles frequently to ensure characters gain a variety of bonuses.
2. Focus on titles that align with your current needs—defensive boosts for dungeons, offensive boosts for bosses.
3. Complete skits, side quests, and combat challenges to unlock hidden titles.

Mastering New Abilities

As your party levels up and earns titles, they'll gain access to powerful new artes. These abilities are crucial for adapting to stronger enemies and more complex battles. Some key abilities unlocked in this chapter include:

Asbel's Rising Falcon: A high-damage arte that combines mobility with a devastating attack.

Sophie's Photon Blaze: A light-element arte effective against dark-aligned enemies.

Pascal's Explosion Nova: A high-powered spell that deals massive fire damage to multiple targets.

Eleth Mixer Upgrades

Chapter 3 introduces opportunities to expand and upgrade the Eleth Mixer, increasing its capacity and efficiency. The Eleth Mixer can now generate rare items, providing a critical edge in challenging battles. Be sure to equip recipes for HP and CC recovery items to keep your party well-sustained during prolonged encounters.

Combat Challenges and Training

Enemies in Chapter 3 are noticeably stronger, with more advanced attack patterns and elemental resistances. This is an ideal time to practice chaining combos, dodging, and guarding effectively. Utilize the following strategies:

Exploit Weaknesses: Study enemy types and equip artes that counter their resistances.

Optimize Party Roles: Assign each character a specific focus, such as crowd control, healing, or sustained damage.

Practice Artes Chains: Learn how to seamlessly link A-Artes and B-Artes to maximize damage output.

Preparation for Fodra's Core
The abilities and titles unlocked in this chapter are essential for tackling the challenges within Fodra's Core, a high-difficulty dungeon that demands precise combat execution. Spend time leveling up and mastering artes to ensure your party is ready for the trials ahead.

Exploring the Fodra Region: Hidden Secrets

The Fodra region is a fascinating and perilous new area that combines breathtaking landscapes with deep lore, offering players a chance to delve into the mysteries of Ephinea's past. This part of the game challenges players to explore uncharted territory, solve puzzles, and uncover hidden treasures, all while facing formidable enemies.

Fodra's Environments and Unique Features
Fodra's terrain is incredibly diverse, ranging from lush bioluminescent forests to desolate, metallic wastelands influenced by ancient technology. These contrasting environments reflect the region's dual nature: a place of both natural beauty and technological decay. Pay close attention to the details in the environment, as many areas

feature visual clues that point to hidden paths, treasures, or skits.

Key areas include:
Fodra's Caverns: A maze of glowing crystals and underground streams, filled with rare crafting materials and dangerous elemental creatures.
The Ruined City: A haunting reminder of a once-thriving civilization, where you'll find critical story revelations and challenging enemy encounters.
Overgrown Lab: A mix of nature and machinery, this area provides insight into Fodra's advanced technological history while housing powerful enemies guarding rare loot.

Hidden Secrets and Side Quests
Fodra is packed with hidden secrets waiting to be discovered. Some notable opportunities include:
Ancient Artifacts: Scattered throughout the region are relics tied to the story of Lambda and Fodra's downfall. Collecting these artifacts often rewards new titles or key story skits.
Treasure Hunts: Keep an eye out for sparkling spots on the ground, which often indicate hidden treasure chests containing powerful equipment, artes tomes, or Eleth Mixer expansions.
Lost Travelers: In some areas, you'll encounter stranded NPCs who offer side quests. These quests not only

provide valuable rewards but also flesh out the lore of the Fodra region.

Navigating Environmental Challenges

Fodra's natural and artificial hazards add layers of complexity to exploration:

Toxic Zones: Certain areas are shrouded in poisonous mist, which drains HP over time. Equip resistance items or artes to mitigate the damage while navigating these zones.

Puzzles and Mechanisms: Many paths are blocked by ancient machinery or overgrown vegetation. Use switches, light beams, and other environmental tools to clear the way.

Hidden Passages: Some walls and platforms are illusory or hidden in plain sight. Interact with suspicious-looking structures to uncover secret paths.

Enemies in Fodra

The creatures in Fodra are significantly tougher, often combining elemental attacks with advanced AI patterns. Key enemies include:

Crystal Guardians: Elemental constructs that are immune to physical attacks but weak to specific artes.

Fodra Predators: Agile beasts with high attack speed, requiring precise dodging and crowd control tactics.

Mutated Behemoths: Large and heavily armored foes that test your party's endurance and teamwork.

Tips for Successful Exploration
1. Plan Your Party Setup*: Use characters with versatile artes to handle the variety of enemy types in the region.
2. Stock Up on Supplies: Bring plenty of healing gels and antidotes to counteract the hazards of the toxic zones.
3. Keep an Eye on Titles: Equip titles that grant bonuses to elemental resistance, as many enemies exploit weaknesses in this chapter.
4. Save Often: Use save points strategically, especially before venturing into areas with tougher enemies or puzzles.

The Fodra region is a treasure trove of secrets and lore, providing vital pieces of the story and equipping your party with the tools they'll need to confront the challenges ahead. Thorough exploration will reward both your curiosity and your combat readiness.

Dungeon Guide: Fodra's Core

Fodra's Core is one of the most challenging dungeons in Tales of Graces F, serving as the climax of the Fodra region's story arc. This labyrinthine dungeon combines intricate puzzles, tough enemy encounters, and intense environmental hazards, all leading to a showdown with

Lambda. Mastering this area requires careful preparation, strategy, and attention to detail.

Entering Fodra's Core
Before venturing into Fodra's Core, ensure your party is fully prepared:
Stock Up on Supplies: Purchase plenty of healing items, gels, and life bottles. The Eleth Mixer should be equipped with recipes for automatic healing during combat.
Equip Resistance Gear: Enemies in Fodra's Core frequently use elemental attacks. Accessories that boost resistance to fire, ice, and lightning are especially useful.
Save Progress: Use the save point near the dungeon entrance and make frequent saves as you progress.

Layout and Puzzles
Fodra's Core is divided into multiple levels, with each section featuring unique challenges:
1. Energy Gates: The first obstacle involves activating energy gates by redirecting power through a series of conduits. This puzzle requires players to manipulate switches and pathways to restore energy flow to blocked doors.
2. Moving Platforms: Later sections include moving platforms over bottomless pits. Timing is critical here, as enemies may ambush you mid-puzzle, forcing you to juggle combat and navigation.

3. Crystal Arrays: Certain paths are sealed by crystalline barriers. To proceed, locate and destroy the source crystals, which are guarded by powerful minibosses.

Enemies in Fodra's Core

The dungeon is home to some of the game's toughest enemies, each requiring specific tactics to defeat:

Elemental Sentinels: These foes use devastating area-of-effect spells. Interrupt their casting by targeting them with stagger-inducing artes.

Fodra Guardians: Large, heavily armored enemies resistant to physical attacks. Use magic artes and ranged attacks to wear them down.

Corrupted Beasts: These enemies deal high damage and often come in packs. Focus on crowd control to keep them from overwhelming your party.

Treasure and Rewards

Fodra's Core is filled with hidden treasures that provide essential upgrades and bonuses:

Rare Equipment: Look for hidden paths and optional minibosses guarding high-tier weapons and armor.

Titles and Artes Tomes: Completing puzzles and defeating minibosses often rewards characters with unique titles or tomes that unlock advanced artes.

Eleth Mixer Upgrades: Some treasure chests contain items that expand the Eleth Mixer's capacity, allowing for more recipes and greater combat support.

Preparing for the Final Boss

At the end of the dungeon, players face Lambda's Awakening, the climactic boss battle of this chapter. To prepare:

Heal your party at the final save point.

Equip gear that boosts elemental resistance, as Lambda uses multiple elemental attacks.

Ensure your Eleth Gauge is full for maximum damage output during Eleth Burst.

Fodra's Core is a test of everything you've learned so far, from strategic combat to puzzle-solving. Take your time exploring, mastering its mechanics, and preparing for the ultimate confrontation that awaits at its heart.

Boss Battle: Lambda's Awakening

The final confrontation of Chapter 3 takes place in Fodra's Core, where the party faces off against Lambda, the entity whose influence has caused chaos throughout the story. This intense boss battle is a test of endurance, strategy, and teamwork, and serves as a critical turning point in the narrative.

Setting the Stage

The arena is a dramatic and ominous space, surrounded by pulsating energy fields and remnants of Fodra's advanced technology. Lambda's form is both imposing and otherworldly, reflecting its immense power and corrupted nature. As the battle begins, tension is heightened by the stakes: the fate of Fodra and Ephinea hinges on your victory.

Boss Details
Name: Lambda
HP: Extremely high, requiring consistent damage and sustained effort.
Phases:The battle is divided into three distinct phases, each introducing new abilities and increasing in difficulty.
Weaknesses:Certain elemental artes can interrupt Lambda's attacks, though these vary between phases.
Strengths:Lambda is resistant to most physical attacks and can nullify some elemental artes, forcing you to adapt your strategy.

Lambda's Abilities and Moveset

Phase 1:
Dark Slash: A powerful melee combo that targets the nearest character. Guard or evade to avoid heavy damage.

Energy Wave: Lambda sends out a wave of dark energy in a straight line. Keep your party spread out to minimize impact.

Summon Minions: Lambda calls forth smaller enemies to distract your party and divide your attention. Eliminate them quickly to focus on the boss.

Phase 2:

Elemental Barrage: Lambda cycles through fire, ice, and lightning-based attacks, targeting random areas of the battlefield. Watch for visual cues to dodge these powerful AoE attacks.

Gravity Well: A large circular attack that draws party members toward the center, dealing damage over time. Use ranged artes or flee the area to avoid being caught.

Heal Regeneration: Lambda periodically heals a portion of its HP, prolonging the fight. Interrupt this ability with stagger-inducing artes.

Phase 3:

Final Surge: Lambda unleashes a devastating ultimate attack that affects the entire battlefield. Guard and use healing artes immediately after to recover.

Rapid Teleportation: Lambda teleports unpredictably, striking party members from unexpected angles. Assign a frontline fighter to keep its attention while others attack from a distance.

Strategy to Win

1. Exploit Weaknesses

In each phase, observe Lambda's attack patterns to identify weaknesses. Use elemental artes that counter its abilities while avoiding those it resists.

2. Prioritize Healing

Keep Sophie or Cheria focused on healing throughout the battle. Use group healing artes and items like Life Bottles to keep your party alive during intense phases.

3. Focus Fire on Lambda

While Lambda summons minions during the fight, these should only be dealt with if they pose an immediate threat. Concentrate your attacks on Lambda to avoid prolonging the battle unnecessarily.

4. Utilize Eleth Burst

Activate Eleth Burst when your gauge is full to unleash uninterrupted combos. This is especially useful during the second and third phases to deal significant damage while avoiding counterattacks.

5. Rotate Artes and Titles

Adapt your artes and titles as the battle progresses. Equip titles that enhance elemental resistance or increase damage output for maximum effectiveness.

Victory and Rewards

Defeating Lambda is a monumental achievement that rewards you with:

A significant experience boost, leveling up all party members.

Rare equipment and accessories that enhance elemental resistance and damage.

Titles for Asbel and Sophie, granting access to powerful new artes.

Aftermath

The victory over Lambda is bittersweet, as it reveals deeper truths about the entity's origin and its connection to Fodra's history. This battle sets the stage for the emotional and narrative developments in the chapters to come, as the party grapples with the consequences of their actions and prepares for the final confrontation with the greater threat ahead.

Chapter 4: Side Quests and Exploration

Optional Bosses and Secret Locations

Chapter 4 of Tales of Graces F shifts focus to optional content, giving players the chance to explore the game's world more thoroughly, uncover secret locations, and challenge powerful optional bosses. These activities not only provide additional rewards but also enrich the lore and offer opportunities to strengthen your party before advancing the main storyline.

Optional Bosses
Optional bosses are scattered throughout the world, each offering unique challenges and high-value rewards.

These bosses are significantly tougher than regular enemies and even some story bosses, requiring careful preparation and strategy.

1. Rockgagong
Location: Strahta Desert
Details: A massive, ancient creature that serves as one of the toughest optional bosses in the game. The Rockgagong's size and strength make this fight a test of endurance.
Rewards: Unique equipment and materials for crafting high-tier weapons.
Strategy: Focus on its weak points, use ranged attacks to avoid its devastating AoE stomps, and keep your healer active throughout the battle.

2. Fodra Queen
Location: Hidden area in Fodra's Core
Details: A powerful entity tied to the region's lore. This boss deals massive elemental damage, requiring strong resistance gear and precise timing.
Rewards: Rare titles and artes tomes for your party.
Strategy: Exploit its weakness to light-based attacks while maintaining a spread-out formation to avoid AoE spells.

3. Abyssal Phantom

Location: Secret cave near Barona Details: A shadowy figure with lightning-fast attacks. This boss tests your ability to guard and counter effectively.
Rewards: High-level armor and an Eleth Mixer upgrade.
Strategy: Time your guards perfectly to stagger the boss, then unleash combos during its recovery.

Secret Locations

Exploration in Tales of Graces F rewards curiosity, with hidden areas scattered across the world. These locations often contain rare treasures, lore insights, and even new titles.

1. The Forgotten Cavern How to Access: Look for a hidden entrance in the Strahta Desert, marked by a faintly glowing symbol.
Contents: Treasure chests with rare crafting materials and a unique accessory that boosts elemental resistance.

2. Sanctuary of Eternity How to Access: Unlock this area by completing a side quest chain in Gralesyde.
Contents: A challenging miniboss and a tome that unlocks a powerful arte for Asbel.

3. Crystal Cove
How to Access: Found in a remote area near the Windor region's coastline. Requires a specific artifact to open.

Contents: Skits that reveal additional lore about Sophie's origins and a high-tier weapon for Pascal.

Tips for Success
1. Prepare Thoroughly: Optional bosses and secret areas are designed for experienced players. Level up your party, equip the best gear available, and stock up on items before attempting these challenges.
2. Explore Carefully: Pay attention to subtle environmental cues, such as unusual markings or paths that seem inaccessible. Interact with NPCs to gather hints about hidden locations.
3. Revisit Old Areas: Many secret locations only become accessible after certain story events. Revisit earlier regions with new abilities to uncover previously hidden treasures.

Exploring these optional areas and defeating powerful bosses not only strengthens your party but also adds depth to the world of Tales of Graces F. These activities are perfect for players who want to fully experience everything the game has to offer.

Collecting Titles and Skits

In Tales of Graces F, titles and skits are integral to the game's charm and depth, offering both gameplay advantages and narrative enrichment. Chapter 4 provides an excellent opportunity to focus on collecting titles and unlocking skits, allowing players to enhance their characters' abilities while deepening their connection to the story and its characters.

Collecting Titles
Titles are more than just cosmetic achievements; they grant stat boosts, unlock artes, and offer unique perks as they level up. Chapter 4 introduces new ways to earn titles, encouraging players to explore and experiment with different aspects of the game.

1. Battle Challenges
Description: Earn titles by defeating specific enemies, achieving high combo counts, or executing perfect guards. For example:
Combo Virtuoso: Land a 50+ hit combo in battle
Guardian of the Field: Successfully guard against 20 attacks in a single fight.
Tip: Experiment with different party combinations to achieve these objectives efficiently.

2. Side Quests and Exploration
Description: Many titles are hidden behind side quests or tied to specific locations. NPCs in towns and remote areas often provide hints or tasks that lead to new titles.

Example: Helping a merchant in Strahta unlocks the Merchant's Ally title for Malik, which boosts his Eleth Mixer effectiveness.

3. Event-Based Titles
Description: Some titles are awarded during significant story events or after completing optional boss battles.
Example: Defeating the Rockgagong grants Asbel the Beast Slayer title, enhancing his physical damage.

Unlocking and Viewing Skits
Skits are short, optional dialogues between characters that reveal their thoughts, relationships, and humorous moments. These skits are triggered by specific events, locations, or gameplay milestones and provide additional context to the story.

1. Environmental Skits
Description: These skits are triggered when exploring certain locations, such as a hidden cavern or a bustling town square.
Example: Visiting the Sanctuary of Eternity unlocks a skit where the group reflects on their journey and Sophie's evolving identity.

2. Combat-Based Skits

Description: Performing specific actions in battle, such as using a certain arte or achieving a high combo, can unlock skits.

Example: Repeatedly using Asbel's Lightning Strike triggers a skit about his obsession with perfecting his technique.

3. Title-Related Skits

Description: Some skits are tied to earning or equipping specific titles. These provide humorous or insightful commentary on the characters' growth.

Example: Equipping Pascal with a crafting-related title might unlock a skit where she jokes about her "mad scientist" tendencies.

Maximizing Titles and Skits

1. Rotate Titles Regularly: To fully utilize titles, switch them frequently to unlock artes and stat bonuses. Focus on leveling up titles that align with your current gameplay goals, such as damage output, healing, or elemental resistance.
2. Explore Thoroughly: Many skits and titles are tied to specific locations or NPC interactions. Revisit old areas and speak to townsfolk to uncover hidden opportunities.
3. Use Skit Viewer: Missed a skit? The Skit Viewer in the game's main menu allows you to replay unlocked skits, ensuring you don't miss out on any character moments.

Titles and skits enhance both gameplay and storytelling, rewarding players who take the time to explore every aspect of the game. By focusing on these elements in Chapter 4, you'll gain a deeper appreciation for the characters and their journey while unlocking powerful abilities for future battles.

Maximizing the Eleth Mixer and Dualizing System

The Eleth Mixer and Dualizing System are two core gameplay mechanics in Tales of Graces F that offer immense versatility in combat, crafting, and resource management. Chapter 4 provides an excellent opportunity to master these systems, ensuring your party is well-prepared for the challenges ahead.

Eleth Mixer: An Essential Tool
The Eleth Mixer is a unique feature that allows players to generate items, recover health, and activate bonuses during combat or exploration. It operates on Eleth Points (EP), which deplete as the mixer functions.

How to Use the Eleth Mixer Effectively

1. Set Useful Recipes

Equip recipes for items like Apple Gels, Panacea Bottles, and TP recovery gels. These items will automatically activate during combat when certain conditions are met.

Example: Assign a recipe for Life Bottles to ensure automatic revival if a party member falls in battle.

2. Generate Rare Items

The mixer can also create rare materials and crafting components during exploration. Recipes for ingredients like Arcane Crystals or Magical Herbs are particularly valuable.

Example: Equip a recipe for Rare Metal while exploring Fodra's Core to gather crafting materials for powerful weapons.

3. Upgrade the Mixer

As you progress, you'll find items that expand the Eleth Mixer's capacity, allowing you to set more recipes and hold additional EP. Seek out these upgrades in treasure chests or as rewards for defeating optional bosses.

Tips for Maximizing EP Efficiency

Conserve EP by limiting the number of active recipes during regular exploration and reserving high-cost recipes for boss fights.

Refill EP at inns or with special items when needed.

Dualizing System: Crafting and Upgrades

The Dualizing System allows players to combine items to create new weapons, armor, accessories, and consumables. It's a vital tool for strengthening your party and tailoring gear to suit specific encounters.

How Dualizing Works

1. Combine Materials Dualizing requires two items: a base item (e.g., a weapon or armor) and a material (e.g., crystals or shards). The result is a more powerful version of the base item.
Example: Combine a Steel Sword with a Sharp Fang to create a Flaming Sword, which deals additional fire damage.

2. Enhance Accessories
Accessories can be dualized to provide elemental resistances or bonus stats.
 Example: Dualizing an Amulet with an Elemental Stone grants resistance to lightning-based attacks.

3. Create Consumables
You can also dualize consumables, such as combining herbs and gels to produce unique healing items.

Key Dualizing Recipes

Weapons: Upgrade base weapons with elemental shards to create gear tailored to specific enemies.

Armor: Focus on dualizing armor to increase resistance to elemental attacks in areas like Fodra's Core.

Accessories: Experiment with combinations to boost stats or add unique effects, such as auto-healing.

Tips for Mastering the Systems

1. Experiment Freely: Dualizing allows for creativity, so don't hesitate to try different combinations. The game's crafting menu provides previews of potential results, making experimentation risk-free.
2. Prioritize Elemental Gear: Tailor your equipment to counter the elemental strengths of enemies in upcoming areas.
3. Sell Unneeded Items: Dualized items often fetch higher prices at shops, providing an excellent source of income for restocking essentials.
4. Balance Mixer and Dualizing: Use the Eleth Mixer to generate materials that can be dualized, ensuring a steady supply of crafting resources.

Mastering the Eleth Mixer and Dualizing System not only enhances your party's effectiveness in battle but also allows for greater customization and resource management. By investing time in these systems, you'll gain a significant edge in both combat and exploration as the story continues.

Chapter 5: The Lineage and Legacies Arc

Uncovering the Mysteries of Asbel's Heritage

The Lineage and Legacies Arc delves deep into Asbel Lhant's family history, uncovering secrets that shape his identity and role in the unfolding conflict. This segment is rich in narrative revelations, blending emotional storytelling with impactful gameplay moments.

Discovering the Truth About the Lhant Family
As the chapter begins, Asbel is drawn into a series of events that reveal long-buried truths about the Lhant family's connection to Windor's political struggles and the ancient entity, Lambda. Through dialogues, skits, and

exploration, Asbel learns of his father's hidden efforts to safeguard the region from the influences of Lambda and Fodra's technology. These revelations challenge Asbel to reconcile his memories of his father with the man who bore the weight of protecting Lhant.

Key Events in the Arc
1. Returning to Lhant
Revisiting the Lhant Manor triggers a sequence where Asbel uncovers his father's journals and hidden artifacts. These items provide insight into Lord Aston's involvement in the research of ancient Fodran technology and his alliance with key figures in Windor's history.

2. Sophie's Connection
Asbel's discoveries deepen his understanding of Sophie's origins, tying her to the ancient experiments conducted on Fodra. This connection raises questions about her role in the battle against Lambda and her place within the group.

3. The Lhant Emblem
A pivotal moment occurs when Asbel receives the Lhant Emblem, a symbol of his family's legacy and his newfound responsibility. This event strengthens his resolve to protect his friends and face the growing threat of Lambda.

Gameplay Elements

1. Exploration and Skits

Exploring Lhant and surrounding areas reveals additional skits that provide character insights, particularly focusing on Asbel's evolving relationship with Sophie, Cheria, and Hubert.

2. Side Quests

Several optional quests tie into Asbel's heritage, such as helping villagers restore landmarks connected to the Lhant family or uncovering ancient Fodran relics. Completing these quests rewards titles and rare equipment.

3. Title Unlocks

Asbel gains new titles tied to his heritage, such as Lhant Protector, which boosts his defensive capabilities and unlocks artes like Guardian Blade.

Themes and Emotional Impact

This portion of the story emphasizes themes of legacy, responsibility, and the importance of forging one's path. Asbel's journey to understand his family's past parallels his growth as a leader and protector, making this arc a turning point in both the narrative and his character development.

Final Dungeons: Velanik and Barona Catacombs

The final dungeons of Chapter 5, Velanik and Barona Catacombs, bring players to the edge of the narrative climax. These locations are filled with challenging enemies, intricate puzzles, and vital story revelations, leading directly to the final confrontations of the arc.

Velanik: A Ruined Fortress
Velanik is an ancient stronghold that once served as a defense point for the Windor Kingdom. Now abandoned and overtaken by corrupted forces, it serves as the first of two major dungeons in this chapter.

Key Features of Velanik
1. Maze-Like Layout
Velanik is divided into multiple levels, connected by crumbling staircases, hidden passages, and collapsing bridges.
 Players must locate and activate ancient mechanisms to open gates and repair pathways.

2. Environmental Hazards
 Poison traps and falling debris are common throughout the dungeon. Equip accessories that provide resistance to poison and increase evasion to avoid unnecessary damage.

3. Enemies

Velanik's foes include armored soldiers and spectral entities tied to the fortress's dark history.

Notable enemy types:

Ghost Knights: Resistant to physical attacks but weak to light-based artes.

Corrupted Archers: Attack from a distance; take them out quickly to avoid interruptions during combat.

4. Treasure and Rewards

Hidden chests contain high-tier weapons and armor. Look for breakable walls and floor switches to uncover secret rooms.

Completing optional puzzles rewards players with arte tomes and Eleth Mixer expansions.

Barona Catacombs: The Underground Graveyard

The Barona Catacombs lie beneath the Windor capital, acting as the final dungeon before the chapter's climactic battles. These ancient tunnels house the remnants of Lambda's growing influence and contain vital story revelations.

Key Features of Barona Catacombs

1. Dark and Ominous Atmosphere

Dimly lit corridors and eerie music set the tone for this dungeon. Players will encounter remnants of the catacombs' past, including inscriptions and skeletal remains.

2. Puzzles and Pathways

The catacombs require players to solve intricate light-reflection puzzles to open gates and proceed.
Some paths are blocked by debris and require players to locate hidden switches or defeat minibosses to clear the way.

3. Enemies

The catacombs are infested with Lambda-corrupted creatures, making the battles here particularly intense.
Notable enemy types:
Shadow Beasts: Agile and powerful, they deal heavy damage but are vulnerable to light artes.
Wraith Lords: Minibosses that guard critical pathways, capable of summoning additional enemies to aid them.

4. Save Points and Healing

Strategically placed save points allow players to heal and prepare for upcoming encounters. Use them wisely to adjust party tactics and replenish resources.

Preparation for the Boss Battles

At the end of the Barona Catacombs, players face the first major boss, Emeraude, setting the stage for Lambda's final form. Before proceeding:

Equip Elemental Resistance Gear: Both Velanik and the catacombs feature enemies with elemental attacks, so gear tailored to specific elements will be crucial.

Optimize Artes and Titles: Equip titles that maximize damage output or provide defensive boosts for the bosses ahead.

Stock Up on Supplies: Ensure your inventory is filled with gels, life bottles, and TP recovery items.

These dungeons are a test of everything you've learned so far, combining intense combat with narrative depth to prepare you for the final confrontation.

Boss Battles: Emeraude and Lambda's Final Form

The culmination of Chapter 5 features two intense and emotional boss battles: Emeraude and Lambda's Final Form. These battles test your mastery of combat mechanics, party management, and strategic thinking while delivering some of the most dramatic moments in Tales of Graces F.

Boss Battle: Emeraude

Emeraude, a key figure in the narrative, reveals her true motives and serves as the penultimate challenge before the final confrontation with Lambda. Her abilities reflect her mastery of technology and dark magic, making her a formidable opponent.

Battle Overview

HP: High, requiring sustained damage and strategic resource management.

Weakness: Vulnerable to light-based artes.

Strengths: Resistant to physical attacks and dark-element artes.

Abilities and Moveset

1. Dark Pulse: An AoE attack that deals significant dark-element damage to all party members. Keep your party spread out to minimize its impact.
2. Energy Barrage: Emeraude fires multiple projectiles that track party members. Dodge or guard to avoid being overwhelmed.
3. Summon Drones: She periodically summons drones that assist her in battle, attacking with ranged energy blasts.
4. Void Shield: Emeraude activates a shield that absorbs damage temporarily. Use this time to heal and reposition.
5. Cataclysm Wave (Ultimate Move): A devastating attack that covers the entire battlefield. Guard and immediately heal afterward.

Strategy

1. Prioritize the Drones: Eliminate the summoned drones quickly to avoid being overwhelmed by their ranged attacks.

2. Exploit Weaknesses: Use light-element artes and ranged attacks to chip away at Emeraude's health while avoiding her counterattacks.
3. Guard and Heal: Guard during her ultimate move and ensure Sophie or Cheria is focused on healing the party throughout the fight.
4. Utilize Eleth Burst: Save your Eleth Burst for when her Void Shield is down to deal uninterrupted damage.

Victory Rewards

Defeating Emeraude rewards the party with rare materials, an Eleth Mixer upgrade, and powerful arte tomes that prepare them for the final battle.

Boss Battle: Lambda's Final Form

The battle against Lambda is the ultimate test of your skills and serves as the emotional and narrative climax of Chapter 5. Lambda has fully awakened, and its form embodies raw power and darkness, posing a multi-phase challenge.

Battle Overview

HP: Massive across multiple phases.

Weakness: Changes with each phase, requiring adaptability.

Strengths: High resistance to physical attacks and a wide range of elemental artes.

Abilities and Moveset

Phase 1:
Energy Slash: A powerful melee combo that targets the closest character.
Void Rain: Lambda rains dark energy bolts over the battlefield. Move constantly to avoid damage.
Summon Shadows: Summons shadow clones to assist in battle.

Phase 2:
Elemental Barrage: Alternates between fire, ice, and lightning attacks in rapid succession.
Gravity Pull: Creates a vortex that draws party members to a central point, followed by an explosive AoE attack.
Regeneration: Lambda restores a portion of its health periodically.

Phase 3:
Chaos Nova: An ultimate move that unleashes a massive explosion, dealing damage to the entire party.
Rapid Teleportation: Lambda teleports unpredictably, targeting party members with devastating strikes.
Overdrive Mode: Lambda enters a berserk state, increasing its attack speed and damage output.

Strategy
1. Adapt to Each Phase: Monitor Lambda's weaknesses and adjust your artes and tactics accordingly.

2. Focus on Healing and Defense: Keep Sophie or Cheria dedicated to healing, and use defensive artes to mitigate Lambda's high-damage attacks.

3. Spread Out the Party: Avoid grouping characters to reduce the impact of AoE attacks.

4. Interrupt Regeneration: Use stagger-inducing artes during Phase 2 to interrupt Lambda's healing attempts.

5. Save Eleth Burst for Phase 3: Unleash your strongest combos during Lambda's berserk state to deal maximum damage while avoiding counters.

Victory Rewards

Defeating Lambda's Final Form unlocks powerful story artefacts, new titles for the entire party, and access to post-game content. This victory is a significant milestone, resolving major plot threads and setting up the final chapters of the game.

Chapter 6: Post-Game Content and Extras

The "Future Arc" Exclusive Content

The "Future Arc" in Tales of Graces F is an additional storyline introduced in the enhanced version of the game. Acting as an extended epilogue, it expands upon the main narrative, offering deeper insight into Sophie's origins, the aftermath of the battle with Lambda, and the evolving dynamics of Asbel's group. This arc provides a fresh adventure with new challenges, characters, and locations to explore.

Story Overview

The Future Arc begins shortly after the conclusion of the main story. Asbel and his companions, now free from the immediate threat of Lambda, must face a new danger stemming from Fodra's remnants. This storyline dives into themes of identity and purpose, particularly focusing on Sophie's relationship with the party and her quest to understand her existence.

Exclusive Features
1. New Areas to Explore
 The Future Arc introduces unique regions within Fodra, including lush biomes and advanced technological ruins that reflect the planet's complex history.
Each area features intricate puzzles and tougher enemies, making exploration both rewarding and challenging.

2. Character Development
The Future Arc explores the emotional growth of the party, with a special focus on Sophie's journey of self-discovery. Interactions between characters deepen, with heartfelt skits and dialogues adding layers to their relationships.

3. New Boss Battles
Face exclusive bosses with unique mechanics and higher difficulty levels. These encounters test your understanding of the game's combat system, rewarding persistence and strategy.

4. Enhanced Artes and Titles

The Future Arc unlocks new artes and titles for each character, further diversifying their combat abilities. For example, Asbel gains *Celestial Blade, a powerful arte with both offensive and defensive utility.

Gameplay Tips for the Future Arc

1. Carry Over Progress

Before starting the Future Arc, ensure you've completed the main story and utilized the Grade Shop to carry over your progress. Carrying over equipment, levels, and titles gives you a significant advantage.

2. Master Advanced Artes

Practice chaining advanced artes and using Eleth Burst strategically. Enemies in the Future Arc are stronger, so mastering combos is essential for victory.

3. Explore Thoroughly

Hidden treasures, rare items, and optional skits are scattered throughout the new areas. Take your time exploring to uncover all the arc has to offer.

Why Play the Future Arc?

The Future Arc is not just an extension of the main story but a vital piece of Tales of Graces F. It provides closure for major characters, answers lingering questions about

Sophie's origin, and introduces exciting gameplay elements that challenge even seasoned players.

Unlocking the Secret Dungeon and Hidden Boss

The post-game Secret Dungeon in Tales of Graces F is a challenging and rewarding experience designed for players looking to test their skills after completing the main story and the Future Arc. It features some of the toughest battles in the game, intricate puzzles, and a powerful hidden boss that serves as the ultimate challenge.

How to Unlock the Secret Dungeon

1. Complete the Future Arc
Finish the Future Arc to unlock hints about the secret dungeon's location and the necessary steps to access it.

2. Locate the Key Item
The entrance to the Secret Dungeon is sealed and requires a special key item to open.
 Clue: Speak with NPCs in major towns like Barona and Gralesyde. They provide cryptic hints about the item's location, often pointing to a hidden area in Fodra.

Tip: Thoroughly explore areas unlocked during the Future Arc, paying attention to glowing symbols or unusual landmarks.

3. Unlock the Entrance
Once you've acquired the key item, head to the dungeon entrance, which is often located in a remote part of Fodra or an ancient ruin tied to Sophie's origin.

Dungeon Features
1. Multi-Level Structure
The dungeon consists of several levels, each with escalating difficulty and unique layouts.
Puzzles: Solve light-reflection challenges, unlock gates by defeating minibosses, and navigate traps like moving platforms and shifting floors.

2. Enhanced Enemies
The dungeon is populated with enhanced versions of regular enemies and exclusive foes with advanced AI and powerful abilities.
Notable Enemy Types:
Ethereal Sentinels: Immune to physical attacks; exploit their elemental weaknesses.
Chaos Beasts: Large creatures that deal massive AoE damage and can stagger your party.

3. Treasure Rooms

Hidden rooms contain high-tier equipment, arte tomes, and Eleth Mixer expansions.
Tip: Look for subtle visual cues, such as cracks in walls or glowing symbols, to locate these hidden areas.

Hidden Boss: The True Guardian

At the dungeon's core lies the ultimate challenge: the True Guardian. This powerful boss tests your mastery of the game's combat mechanics, requiring precise timing, resource management, and adaptability.

Boss Details
HP: Extremely high, with multiple phases.
Abilities:
Elemental Domination: Cycles through fire, ice, lightning, and wind-based attacks. Each phase has different weaknesses and resistances.
Time Warp: Slows or accelerates time, affecting your party's movements and actions.
Ultimate Attack - Celestial Cataclysm: A devastating AoE attack that triggers in the final phase, requiring precise guarding or evasion.

Strategy
1. Exploit Phase Weaknesses

Adapt your artes and tactics for each elemental phase. Equip titles and gear that enhance resistance to the boss's current phase's element.

2. Manage Party Roles

Assign clear roles to each character: damage dealer, healer, and support. Keep your healer positioned safely and prioritize reviving fallen party members.

3. Use Eleth Burst Strategically

Save Eleth Burst for the final phase to unleash uninterrupted combos and deal maximum damage.

4. Stock Up on Items

Bring plenty of healing gels, life bottles, and TP recovery items to sustain your party throughout the prolonged battle.

Rewards

Arte Tomes: Unlock ultimate artes for each character.
Legendary Equipment: The best weapons and armor in the game, tailored for each party member.
Unique Titles: Special titles that grant significant stat boosts and unique abilities.

Strategies for 100% Completion

Achieving 100% completion in Tales of Graces F is a rewarding endeavor for dedicated players. It involves exploring every aspect of the game, from collecting all titles to defeating every optional boss and viewing every skit. This section outlines a comprehensive strategy to help you achieve total mastery of the game.

1. Collecting All Titles

Titles are crucial for unlocking artes, improving stats, and achieving 100% completion. Each character has dozens of titles, many of which require specific conditions to unlock.

Key Tips for Title Collection:
Battle Challenges:
Use a variety of artes in combat to unlock titles related to combo chains, damage dealt, or specific enemy types.
Example: Asbel's Blade Virtuoso title unlocks after achieving a 100+ hit combo.

Side Quests:
Many titles are tied to side quests offered by NPCs in towns and villages. Speak to everyone, revisit areas, and complete these tasks.
Example: Helping a stranded merchant in Strahta unlocks a title for Malik that improves his crafting skills.

Exploration:
Explore hidden areas and dungeons thoroughly. Some titles require finding specific items or interacting with unique objects.

Event-Specific Titles:
Certain titles are tied to story events or optional cutscenes. Be sure to revisit locations and complete the Future Arc for exclusive titles.

2. Viewing All Skits

Skits provide insight into the characters and enrich the story. These are often tied to specific events, locations, or gameplay milestones.

Skit Collection Tips:
Explore Thoroughly: Trigger skits by revisiting key areas after significant story events. Look for the skit prompt in the corner of the screen.
Use the Skit Viewer: The Skit Viewer in the game menu allows you to replay unlocked skits and check which ones you've missed.
Complete Side Quests: Many skits are tied to optional content and specific character interactions.

3. Mastering the Eleth Mixer and Dualizing System

The Eleth Mixer and Dualizing System are essential for crafting rare items and achieving mastery of the game's mechanics.

Tips for Mastery:
Expand the Mixer: Find Eleth Mixer upgrades in treasure chests, side quests, and dungeons. A fully upgraded mixer allows for more recipes and greater efficiency.
Dualize Regularly: Experiment with combinations to craft high-tier weapons, armor, and accessories. Focus on gear that boosts elemental resistance and attack power.
Generate Rare Materials: Use the mixer to generate crafting components required for dualizing legendary equipment.

4. Filling the Enemy Book

The Enemy Bookrequires encountering and defeating every enemy type in the game, including rare and optional bosses.

Tips for Completion:
Revisit Areas: Some enemies only appear during specific story chapters. After completing the game, revisit older areas to find any you missed.

Challenge Optional Bosses: Optional bosses and minibosses often have unique entries in the Enemy Book.

Use Enemy Lures: Certain items increase enemy spawn rates, making it easier to encounter rare creatures.

5. Unlocking Arte Tomes and Advanced Artes

Arte Tomes unlock advanced artes for each character, enhancing their combat abilities and contributing to completion progress.

Tips for Unlocking Artes:

Use Artes Frequently: Consistent use in battle levels up artes and unlocks their advanced versions.

Complete Dungeons: Many arte tomes are hidden in treasure chests or rewarded for completing puzzles in challenging dungeons.

6. Earning Trophies or Achievements

For trophy or achievement hunters, Tales of Graces F offers a range of challenges that require mastery of the game's systems.

Notable Challenges:

Combo King: Achieve a combo chain of 200+ hits.

Crafting Master: Dualize every type of item in the game.

Perfect Completion: Achieve 100% in all categories, including titles, skits, arte tomes, and the Enemy Book.

7. Utilizing the Grade Shop for New Game+

After completing the game, the Grade Shop allows you to carry over progress into a New Game+ playthrough, making it easier to achieve 100% completion.

Recommended Grade Shop Purchases:
Carry Over Titles: Retain all unlocked titles for a significant advantage in combat and exploration.
Double Experience: Level up faster during your second playthrough.
Unlock Skit Viewer: Replay missed skits to ensure full completion.

By following these strategies, you'll be able to experience everything Tales of Graces F has to offer while achieving total mastery of the game. The journey to 100% completion is challenging but immensely rewarding, providing hours of additional gameplay and a deeper appreciation for the world of Ephinea and Fodra.

www.ingramcontent.com/pod-product-compliance
Lightning Source LLC
Chambersburg PA
CBHW070353230526
45471CB00006B/2553